ATHENS

ANDREW LANGLEY

WORLD ALMANAC® LIBRARY

Please visit our web site at: www.worldalmanaclibrary.com
For a free color catalog describing World Almanac® Library's list of high-quality books
and multimedia programs, call 1-800-848-2928 (USA) or 1-800-387-3178 (Canada).
World Almanac® Library's fax: (414) 332-3567.

Library of Congress Cataloging-in-Publication Data

Langley, Andrew.
    Athens / by Andrew Langley.
        p. cm. — (Great cities of the world)
    Includes bibliographical references and index.
    ISBN 0-8368-5021-1 (lib. bdg.)
    ISBN 0-8368-5181-1 (softcover)
    1. Athens (Greece)—Juvenile literature. [1. Athens (Greece).] I. Title. II. Series.
DF917.L36   2003
938'.5—dc22   2003053891

First published in 2004 by
World Almanac® Library
330 West Olive Street, Suite 100
Milwaukee, WI 53212 USA

Copyright © 2004 by World Almanac® Library.

Produced by Discovery Books
Editor: Gianna Williams
Series designers: Laurie Shock, Keith Williams
Designer and page production: Keith Williams
Photo researcher: Rachel Tisdale
Maps and diagrams: Keith Williams
World Almanac® Library editorial direction: Jenette Donovan Guntly
World Almanac® Library editor: Monica Rausch
World Almanac® Library art direction: Tammy Gruenewald
World Almanac® Library production: Beth Meinholz

Photo credits: AKG London: pp.13, 14; AKG London/Erich Lessing: p.11; Art Directors & Trip/A. Dalton: p.35; Art Directors
& Trip/B. Turner: cover, title page, pp.32, 41, 43; Art Directors & Trip/Eric Smith: p.16; Art Directors & Trip/H. Roberts: p.29;
Art Directors & Trip/H. Rogers: pp.4, 8, 18, 20, 24, 27, 33; Art Directors & Trip/T. Bognar: p.19; Chris Fairclough
Photography: pp.21, 22, 25, 28, 42; Corbis: pp.10, 37; Corbis Sygma: p.23; Corbis/Vittoriano Rastelli: p.36; David Simson:
pp.31, 38; Discovery Picture Library: p.12; Getty Images: p.40; Hutchison Library/Nigel Howard: p.7; Hutchison Library/Ron
Giling: p.26

Cover caption: Tourists explore the Parthenon on Athens's Acropolis Hill.

Printed in the United States of America

1 2 3 4 5 6 7 8 9 07 06 05 04 03

Contents

Introduction

Athens is the capital of Greece. It is also by far the largest and most important Greek city and the center of the country's banking, business, education, and industry. It is home to the Greek Parliament and the leader of the Greek Orthodox Church. Nearly thirty percent of the Greek population lives in Athens. Major airports and seaports are nearby.

◄ *Athens is a mix of old and new structures. Here an ancient temple is surrounded by houses, while concrete apartment buildings rise in the distance.*

"Athens, the greatest of cities, and the most famous for wisdom and power."

—Socrates, Greek philosopher, ca. 400 B.C.

Classical Treasures

Athens is a modern and bustling city, but it is celebrated throughout the world for quite a different reason. Every year millions of tourists go to Athens to see the magnificent remains left by a civilization that flourished nearly 2,500 years ago. Athens was the leading city of ancient Greece, whose developments in culture and society have had a great and lasting influence on the way we live today. The Parthenon temple on the Acropolis and other ancient temples and theaters in the city are some of the most famous sights on Earth. Democracy (literally meaning "rule by the people" in Greek) as a system of government was born in ancient Athens, and this system has inspired much of the world ever since.

Modern City

Athens is the cultural heart of Greece, and tourism is one of the most important parts of Athens's economy. Visitors arrive at the new Eleftherios Venizelos Airport or by sea at Piraeus. This seaport is the largest in the country, handling over five million passengers every year. Most of Greece's imported and exported goods also arrive and leave through Piraeus.

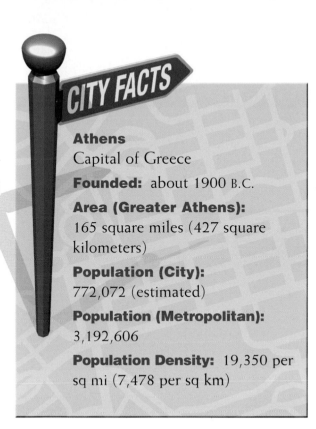

CITY FACTS

Athens
Capital of Greece
Founded: about 1900 B.C.
Area (Greater Athens): 165 square miles (427 square kilometers)
Population (City): 772,072 (estimated)
Population (Metropolitan): 3,192,606
Population Density: 19,350 per sq mi (7,478 per sq km)

Modern Athens is a surprising and exciting mixture of old and new, consisting of a modern city built around and among Athens's ruins. In the past several decades, concrete buildings have replaced many run-down structures, and the number of cars and trucks on the streets has increased, often contributing to traffic jams and air pollution. Meanwhile, archaeologists continue to work carefully to restore the ruins of the ancient city.

Sunny Weather

The city's climate is mainly warm and dry. Athens receives over 2,700 hours of sunshine each year, and the average temperature in summer is about 76° F (24° C). In midsummer, it sometimes gets as

Principal Areas of Athens (Inset of City Center)

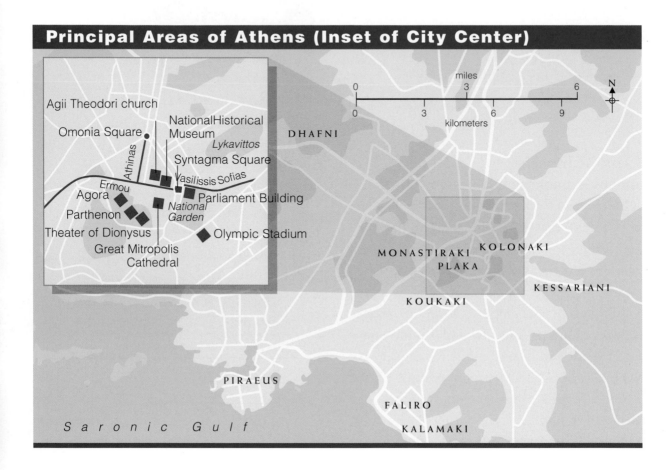

hot as 104° F (40° C). Only 16 inches (400 mm) of rain falls per year, and winter brings only a few days of frost or snow.

A Prime Position

Athens is the chief city of the Attica Region in southeastern Greece. It is set on a peninsula that juts out into the Aegean Sea. The city is only 5 miles (8 kilometers) from the coast of the Saronic Gulf, an inlet of the Aegean. The harbor of Piraeus, located on the coast, is one of the busiest seaports in the eastern Mediterranean.

The city is built on a plain and bordered by mountains to the west, north, and east. These mountains include Hymettos at 3,375 feet (1,029 meters) high, Pendelikón at 3,650 feet (1,110 m), Párnis at 4,645 feet (1,415 m), and Aegaleos at 1,535 feet (468 m).

A High City

Within the city, eight hills rise above the plain. The tallest of these hills is Lykavittos, rising to 910 feet (277 m), but by far the most famous hill is the Acropolis, which means "high city" in Greek. This rocky crag, topped with ancient temples, rises to

512 feet (156 m) and can be seen from almost anywhere in the city center.

Life in Athens revolves around three main squares. Syntagma Square is the center of government and business and is lined with many grand buildings, including the Greek Parliament and other important offices. Omonia Square is the chief shopping area, with modern department stores and restaurants. Monastiraki Square lies at the heart of the old market district and contains many food stalls and other stalls, as well as antique and craft stores.

The city sprawls far outside the ancient center. Greater Athens today measures about 13 miles (21 km) from north to south. Much of this new development, however, is poorly planned, especially in the heavy industrial areas of Piraeus and the Bay of Eleusis to the south and west.

▼ *Piraeus, the main port of Attica, has three harbors. From the harbor shown below, hydrofoil boats called "Flying Dolphins" carry people to the Greek islands.*

CHAPTER 1

History of Athens

By 1900 B.C. a Greek-speaking people had settled in Athens. The area's flat land and its location near the sea made it an ideal place for a settlement. Also, and perhaps more importantly, the Acropolis Hill was a perfect stronghold against enemies, with its steep sides and freshwater springs. At first the city of Athens was limited just to the Acropolis Hill. From the top it was easy to spot anyone approaching by land or sea. In about 1400 B.C. the Greeks built a fortress on the Acropolis.

Greece at this time was not a single nation but rather a geographic area in which city-states governed themselves. Athens was one such city-state. City-states often went to war against each other or formed alliances with other city-states to fight wars.

The Acropolis

The Acropolis Hill dominates the city of Athens. Sights on the Acropolis are open throughout the year and are often covered with tourists, especially in summer. The entrance to the sights is from the west through the Beule Gate above the Agora, the ancient Athenian market square. Upon entering, the Propylaia (the original entrance hall) is to the left and beyond it the Erechtheum, a temple dedicated to Athena, the patron goddess of Athens, featuring statues of women called caryatids (left). The Sacred Way leads eastward to the Parthenon temple and, in the far east corner, the Acropolis Museum.

Kings and Tyrants

Athens was originally ruled by kings, but by about 650 B.C., the wealthier citizens of Athens were electing the rulers, called archons. This system, however, gave no rights to ordinary people and the poor. The situation led to civil unrest, and in 580 B.C. an army commander called Peisistratos seized power and became the city's first tyrant. Peisistratos made several reforms in government and was supported by the lower classes. His son Hippias, however, ruled Athens harshly and was eventually overthrown.

The Birth of Democracy

In 508 B.C. Cleisthenes, "the law-giver," established a form of democracy in Athens. All men over eighteen were registered as citizens, with equal rights, and divided into ten tribes. Each tribe appointed fifty members to a council of five hundred men, which ran the city's government. Every citizen was allowed to vote on major decisions. This system of democracy was still unjust in some ways — women and slaves, for example, could not vote — but it greatly increased the number of people who could participate in government. It has been copied and adapted in various forms ever since.

At this time Athens was still a medium-sized city with few major buildings, but it was growing into one of Greece's most powerful city-states.

Persia launched an attack on Athens in 490 B.C., but the Athenians were able to beat the Persians in a battle at Marathon in Attica. Ten years later, the Persians returned. Although they reached Athens and destroyed the city, the Athenians had already abandoned it. The Athenian navy smashed the Persian fleet at Salamis, near Piraeus, and the citizens returned to Athens victorious. This amazing success made Athens the most powerful city in Greece — and the wealthiest. It was the beginning of the city's "Classical Age."

The Classical Age

Soon after the Persian Wars, in the 450s B.C., Pericles rose to power in Athens. He transformed Athens into one of the main cultural centers of the world. Magnificent new buildings were built on the Acropolis, most notably the Parthenon and the Propylaia. Great writers and artists also lived and worked in the city at this time, including the playwrights Aeschylus and Euripides and the philosopher Socrates.

"We use our wealth in practical ways, rather than simply showing off, and believe that the real disgrace of poverty does not lie in hiding it, but in refusing to struggle against it."

—Thucydides, Athenian historian, ca. 455–399 B.C.

The Classical Age lasted for less than fifty years. In 431 B.C. Athens went to war against its arch-rival Sparta and fought off and on until finally losing in 404 B.C. A long and slow decline of Athen's power and wealth then began. The city was ruled by a series of invaders: the Macedonians, under Alexander the Great, were followed by the

▼ *The Parthenon, on the highest point of the Acropolis, was built as a temple to the goddess Athena. It has eight columns at each end and seventeen on its sides.*

Romans. In A.D. 267 it was overrun by a German tribe, who destroyed many of the buildings. Athenians then built a wall to protect the inner part of the city.

Byzantine Empire
Athens eventually became part of the Byzantine Empire, which was governed from Constantinople (now Istanbul in Turkey). The Byzantine rulers wanted to establish their Christian religion in Athens in place of the old religion and teachings of

Byzantine Churches

Byzantine rule had an enormous effect on Athens, and its effect can clearly be seen today. The main religion is still Greek Orthodox, which developed out of the Byzantine form of Christianity. This religion in turn inspired a new kind of church building, in the shape of a cross covered with a domed roof. Many of these churches exist in the city, most notably Agii Theodori in Klafthmonos Square and the Kapnikarea on Ermou Street. The Byzantine Museum on Vasilissis Sofias Avenue contains many treasures of the Byzantine period.

▼ *This painted wood relief, possibly of St. George, is one of many precious examples of early Christian art in the Byzantine Museum.*

the Greek philosophers. In A.D. 529 the Byzantine emperor Justinian closed the city's universities and schools.

Ottoman Invasion

During the Middle Ages, beginning in about 600, Athens was a ghost town, ruined and forgotten. For much of this time it was ruled by the Byzantine Empire based in Constantinople, although only one emperor ever visited the city. In the 1450s, however, the Byzantines themselves were swept away by a new power—the Ottoman Turks.

The Ottomans entered Athens in 1456 and turned it into a Muslim city. The Parthenon became an Islamic mosque. Many Turks came to live in Athens, but they did little to repair the ruins. More damage was caused in 1687 when

▲ *A Venetian shell explodes in the Parthenon in 1687,*
causing huge damage to the roof, walls, and columns.
It also started a fire that burned for two days.

forces from the Italian city-state of Venice
shelled a store of Turkish gunpowder in
the Parthenon. The building's roof was
blown off.

Fighting for Independence

Eventually even the Ottoman Empire began
to fall apart. As Turkish rule grew weaker,
the Greeks launched their struggle for
independence, helped by the governments
of Great Britain, Russia, and France. In
1821, the Greeks, including the Athenians,
rose in rebellion, took control of Athens and
a peninsula of land nearby called the
Peloponnese, and declared Greece an
independent state. After a long war, the
Turks left Athens for good in 1833.

Greece was finally independent.
Orthodox Christianity replaced Islam once
more, and many mosques became churches.
An alliance of the countries that had
supported Greek independence selected
the kingdom's first ruler, King Otto (or
Otho) of Bavaria (now part of Germany).

In 1834, Greece officially became a monarchy.

Rebuilding the City

King Otto made Athens the new capital of Greece. The city had a falling population, and its buildings and streets were badly damaged by wars and centuries of neglect. Otto started a program of rebuilding, creating elegant new squares and wide, tree-lined avenues. Many of the buildings built during this time have since been knocked down, but some fine ones can still be seen on Vasilissis Sofias Avenue. The Greek National Parliament building, for example, was originally built as Otto's royal palace.

Meanwhile archaeologists began the enormous task of restoring the architectural remains of Classical Athens. Athens grew again into a beautiful and popular place. When the Olympic Games were revived in 1896, the city was chosen to host them. By this time the population had grown rapidly from 31,000 in 1850 to over 111,000.

Twentieth-Century Turmoil

In the early twentieth century, Athens was a quiet and modest-sized city. In 1923, however, Athens experienced a great change. Greece was defeated in another war

▼ Greek independence fighters camp near Athens during the long struggle against Turkish rule. The War of Independence lasted from 1821 to 1833.

with Turkey. Large parts of Greek land became Turkish, and the Greek residents of these lands were sent to Greece. Over 300,000 of them settled in Athens, and new housing areas had to be built for them.

Throughout the twentieth century, several Greek governments were over-thrown and restored in quick succession. Between 1924 and 1935 Greece was a republic. The monarchy was restored in 1935 and a dictatorship established in 1936.

World War II and Beyond

German troops invaded Greece during World War II (1939–1945) and occupied Athens. The oppressive period of occupation was worsened by the harsh winter of 1941-1942, during which some two thousand people died each day of cold, disease, and starvation.

When the Germans left in 1944, another bloody struggle began. Communists wanted to govern the country, but they were opposed by the supporters of the monarchy, backed by British troops. The first battle in the civil war between the two groups took place in Athens when Athenian police shot dead sixteen communist demonstrators. Bullet holes from this war can still be seen in some of the city's walls. The war ended with the communists' defeat in 1949.

Athens finally could begin to rebuild and expand in the 1950s. The city, however, soon experienced further political unrest. In 1964 an anti-royalist, Georgios Papandreou, became prime minister. He was forced to resign a year later by King Constantine II.

Repressive military rule under the so-called "colonels" began in 1967. During this time many poorly constructed houses were built in Athens. In 1973, students at Athens Polytechnic became the first to rebel against the colonels. When the government sent

◀ *A German tank and its crew are stationed beneath the Acropolis. The Germans invaded Greece in 1941 and occupied the capital until 1944.*

The Elgin Marbles

In the early 1800s, foreign visitors came to marvel at the ancient ruins of Athens, some taking parts of the ruins home. Englishman Lord Elgin used levers and other tools to remove many stones from the Acropolis in 1801. The most important of these stones are parts of the Parthenon's carved frieze. Elgin later sold his collection to the British government, and the so-called Elgin Marbles are now on display in the British Museum in London, England. For many years the Greek government has been demanding that the Elgin Marbles be returned to Athens.

tanks in to crush the uprising, over twenty students were killed. That same year, the military government abolished the monarchy of Greece, but by 1974, military rule was over. Greece then became a democratic republic.

In 1981, Andreas Papandreou, son of Georgios Papandreou and head of a left-wing political party, became prime minister of Greece, serving until 1989. Papandreou was the first socialist prime minister. He also served as prime minister from 1993 to 1996.

Athens has had many male mayors, but in October 2002, Athenians elected their first female mayor, Dora Bakoyianni, daughter of former prime minister Constantine Mitsotakis. Bakoyianni served in her father's government as minister of culture.

Terrorism

Like many international cities, Athens has had to deal with the constant threat of terrorism, principally from one organization. The left-wing terrorist group November 17 has carried out attacks since the 1970s (the group is named for the date of the student uprising in 1973). In total it has killed twenty-one people, many of them foreigners, including three U.S. diplomats and the CIA's chief in Athens. Other victims have included the husband of Athens's mayor Dora Bakoyianni and a former governor of the Greek state bank.

In 1999, the November 17 group was responsible for a rocket attack on the home of a German ambassador in Athens. Several members of the group were arrested in July 2002 after a failed bomb attack.

At the Heart of Europe

Since 1981 Greece has been a member of the European Union (E.U.), a political, financial, and industrial alliance of many European countries. January 2002 saw Greece drop its currency, the drachma, in favor of the new European currency, the Euro.

In April 2003 — the year Greece held the presidency of the European Union — delegations from all fifteen member states of the union met in Athens to sign an historic agreement. The Athens Treaty increased the membership of the European Union from fifteen to twenty-five countries.

15

CHAPTER 2

People of Athens

The ancestry of most Greeks is a mixture of the various peoples who have invaded or lived in the region since the beginning of its history. Athenians' ancestry is no exception. Lying on the border between East and West and, by way of the Mediterranean Sea, only a short distance from North Africa, Athens has attracted settlers from all parts of the world.

Pure Greeks?

Athenians like to believe they are descended from the "true" Greeks of ancient Classical times. Since Classical times,

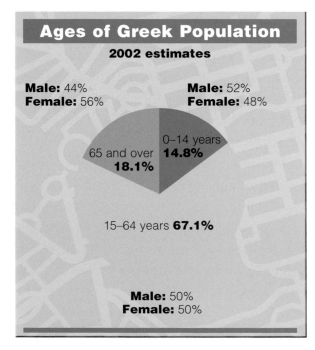

Ages of Greek Population

2002 estimates

Male: 44%
Female: 56%

Male: 52%
Female: 48%

65 and over
18.1%

0–14 years **14.8%**

15–64 years **67.1%**

Male: 50%
Female: 50%

◀ *An Athenian proudly holds his grandchild. Greek children are often named after a saint. Children celebrate their saint's feast day in place of their birthdays.*

however, so many foreigners have ruled the city that no one can really claim to be a "pure" Athenian. Most Athenians are descendants of Germanic peoples, Slavs, Albanians, and other Europeans, as well as Turks and peoples of the Asian Steppes.

Many settlers from other parts of Greece have come to live in the capital over the last one hundred years. Thousands of immigrants also came from Turkey in 1923, when Greece lost some of its territory to Turkey. Since World War II, thousands more have come from poorer mainland villages and from the Greek islands in search of work. Altogether these Greeks from the provinces make up over half of the total population of Athens.

International City

Newcomers continue to arrive in Athens from a wider area than ever before. Russians, Poles, Ukrainians, and Albanians come from the former communist countries. Fleeing war in their homelands, Iranians, Iraqis, and Afghans also have arrived in Athens. Nigerians, Kenyans, Ethiopians, and people from other parts of Africa, often escaping famine and poverty, come to build a new life in the Greek capital.

Athens also has a large population of short-term visitors. Most of these people have come to see and study the wonderful remains of the city's ancient past. Every year at least 8.5 million tourists and students spend time in the city.

It's Greek to Me

Greek is probably the oldest language in Europe. Many everyday English words (such as music, zoo, Olympics, poetry, telephone, atom, *and* alphabet) *are borrowed from Greek ones. The Greek language also has its own alphabet. Some letters appear similar to letters in the English alphabet, but they have different names.*

alpha	α	A	nu	ν	N
beta	β	B	xi	ξ	Ξ
gamma	γ	Γ	omicron	o	O
delta	δ	Δ	pi	π	Π
epsilon	ε	E	rho	ρ	P
zeta	ζ	Z	sigma	σ	Σ
eta	η	H	tau	τ	T
theta	θ	Θ	upsilon	υ	Y
iota	ι	I	phi	φ	Φ
kappa	κ	K	chi	χ	X
lambda	λ	Λ	psi	ψ	Ψ
mu	μ	M	omega	ω	Ω

A Nation's Faith

Nearly all Greeks are Christians belonging to the Greek Orthodox Church. Throughout the whole country, about 97 percent of Greeks are Orthodox, but in Athens the figure is slightly lower because many immigrants and foreigners of different faiths live there. The city is home to small groups of other Christians (Roman Catholics and Protestants), as well as Muslims and Jews.

The Orthodox Church dates back beyond A.D. 1000, when the Christian church divided. The Catholic Church in the west was based in Rome. In the east, the Orthodox (meaning "right-believing") Church was based in Constantinople. The Greek section of the Orthodox Church became a vital part of Greek culture and helped preserve Greek identity and learning during the long Turkish occupation.

Today the Orthodox Church continues to influence the lives of Athenians. Nearly all marriages take place before a priest, churches are full for regular services, and major religious festivals draw enormous crowds of worshippers. The people of Athens have a special bond with their faith because the Archbishop of Athens is also head of the Greek Orthodox Church.

▼ *Children parade through the streets of Athens during a Good Friday procession.*

Festivals

Easter is the most important of the Orthodox festivals. On Easter, Orthodox Christians remember the death and resurrection of Jesus. Solemn processions are held in the streets on Good Friday. On Easter Saturday at midnight all the lights in the churches are put out. Then candles are lit to celebrate Christ's rising from the dead. After midnight, fireworks, dancing, and outdoor feasts begin. On Easter Sunday, people eat eggs dyed red, first cracking the shells against their neighbors'. At midday Athenians feast on lamb roasted on a spit.

Christmas Day is the second most important holiday. Religious services and feasting are held on this day, but the celebrations in Athens are not as great as those in the United States and Europe. In recent years, however, more Westernized decorations and traditions, such as giving presents, have become popular.

Churches of Athens

The largest and grandest Orthodox church in Athens is the cathedral, or Great Mitropolis, in Mitropolis Square (near Syntagma Square). It was built in the mid-nineteenth century, and all of the major festivals are celebrated there. The Little Mitropolis, a small medieval church made of fragments from ancient ruins, stands near the cathedral. Other major churches in Athens include the Kapnikarea, Agii Theodori, and the Metamorphosis.

▲ *The Little Mitropolis, shown here in front of the Great Mitropolis, features inscriptions and reliefs from the Byzantine ruins out of which it was built.*

Other Faiths

St. Paul's Anglican Church, a major Protestant church, stands on Philellion Street in central Athens. Two other Anglican churches are also found in Athens.

About 3,000 Greek Jews live in Athens. The city is home to the Jewish Museum of Greece, which highlights the 2,300-year history of Greek-speaking Jews in the region, as well as their experiences during

German occupation in World War II.

Athenian Muslims can worship at several of the old mosques that remain from the days of Ottoman occupation. One of the most beautiful mosques is Tzistarakis Mosque in Monastiraki Square. The mosque also houses a museum of Greek ceramics.

Greek Cuisine

An appreciation for delicious and relaxing meals lies at the center of Greek society. Mealtimes are occasions to meet and socialize with family and friends. Breakfast, usually eaten between 6:00 and 8:00 A.M., is a simple affair of coffee, bread, and butter. Athenians normally eat lunch between 2:00 and 3:00 P.M., followed by a siesta, or afternoon rest. Dinner is served late, between 9:00 and 11:00 P.M., and is often the main meal of the day.

A Greek dinner is an informal and slow affair. It usually starts with *mezes*, a series of appetizing tidbits including olives, grilled vegetables, and yogurt dips. Appetizers are served next and often feature seafood from the Aegean Sea, cheese made from goat or sheep's milk, and a green salad. The main course might be lamb, simply grilled over a fire, or more fish. Ice cream or fruit are the most popular desserts.

Native Athenians will often drink wine with their meal. They are proud of their local wines and often claim that ancient Greeks were the first people to produce the drink. They rarely drink it, however, outside

CHAPTER 3

Living in Athens

Over the last eighty years, housing in Athens has expanded in great bursts to match sudden increases in the city's population. A wave of 300,000 Greek immigrants arrived in 1923 from Greek lands lost to Turkey. Then, in the 1950s, Greeks from throughout the country arrived in Athens after the upheaval of the civil war. The largest population growth, however, has occurred since the 1970s. Many refugees from the war-torn Balkans and the former communist countries of Eastern Europe have come to settle in Athens.

Housing in Central Athens

Plaka is the oldest area in which to live in central Athens. This area features narrow streets, long flights of steps, courtyards, and modest-sized houses. It is one of the few areas of the city that survived the long years of Turkish rule intact. Other old dwellings and apartments are in nearby Monastiraki. Most dwellings here are cramped and have no backyards, but many places have a balcony or verandah where people can nap during hot afternoons.

Housing in the city center is very limited because much of the space here is used for new hotels, stores, and office buildings, as well as for facilities for a growing number of tourists. Only the wealthy can afford to live

◄ Athens's old city center is surrounded by rings of suburbs and housing developments that have dramatically increased the size of the city.

in the fashionable and exclusive central districts, such as Kolonaki. Many national embassies are also housed in this area.

The Suburbs

The majority of Athenians live in the suburbs that ring the city center. Some of these suburbs are old communities that have been absorbed by the city. Elegant Kifissia and the monastic settlement at Dhafni lie on the northern edge of Athens, while Kessariani is to the east. To the south, along the coast, are the more industrialized areas, such as Glyfada and Kalamaki. Other suburbs are new "green" villages. These villages are near open spaces and have well-planned buildings.

The recent demand for housing, however, has been so huge that developments have been built farther and farther outside the city. Much of the housing in these developments has been cheaply built, without planning agreements or visits from city building inspectors. The results are neighborhoods of concrete apartment buildings, many of which are built dangerously close to industrial sites.

Commuting from the suburbs to work in central Athens is often difficult. Kifissia and the northern areas are served by an electric railroad, making the trip easier. The Athens bus service is also extensive, with stations in Mount Párnis, Kastri, Loutsa, Varkiza, Piraeus, and Dhafni. Public transportation is free during the morning rush hour.

Athens Earthquake

In 1999, an earthquake hit the northern suburbs of Athens. Many houses and apartment buildings, poorly made of reinforced concrete, were damaged or destroyed. Over 70,000 Athenians were left homeless, and 138 people died. Since this disaster, building codes have become stricter. New apartment blocks must be built to a higher standard of safety and strength.

Homelessness

Greater Athens has more than 11,000 homeless people. Of those, 8,000 are foreign immigrants. Many of these people spend their nights sleeping in the streets or in metro passages.

Shopping in Athens

Stores and markets have existed in Athens for at least 3,000 years. The main shopping area for tourists is around Ermou Street, which runs between Syntagma Square and Monastiraki Square. Traffic is now banned from Ermou Street, allowing pedestrians to roam freely. Here people can browse the shops, drink coffee, or listen to the many street musicians. The more expensive shops and department stores lie to the east, while smaller stores and craft workshops are to the west. Minion, a well-known department store, is on nearby Patission Street.

The streets around Monastiraki Square are filled with hardware stores and practical outlets for native Athenians. Every Sunday a flea market, selling everything from tourist souvenirs to inexpensive antiques, is held in the square.

Greeks tend to buy food at traditional markets, such as the old covered market on Athinas Street. This market offers meat and fish stalls on one side and fruit and vegetables stalls on the other. Many city districts also have their own weekly markets selling fresh food and household goods.

▼ *Kolonaki is one of the most expensive areas of the city with its chic clothing stores, restaurants, and art galleries.*

▲ *Traffic has been banned from part of the center of Athens, making life easier for shoppers and sightseers.*

Buying Clothes

Most average Athenians dress similar to people of other major European cities — young people wear jeans and t-shirts, businessmen and women wear suits, and everyday clothes for women consist of simple dresses and sandals. Athenians buy clothes at market stalls or in the growing number of international stores such as Benetton and Versace. Fashionable clothes stores and designer boutiques, mostly centered in Kolonaki Square, cater to more expensive tastes.

Global Goldsmiths

In 1940, when Ilias Lalaounis began to work for his family goldsmith's firm, he also started creating his own innovative jewelry designs. He eventually founded his own business, which has since become one of the most famous goldsmith companies in the world. Lalaounis gold jewelry, often inspired by designs from ancient Greece and the Byzantine era, is highly prized and very expensive. Lalaounis was commissioned to design the torch for the 1992 Olympics. The company now has stores in New York, Paris, Tokyo, Hong Kong, and London, but its first and main outlet (now also a museum) is in Athens.

Older people in Athens still wear more traditional Greek clothing, which consists of black dresses and headscarves for women and black suits with open-necked shirts for men. Many recent immigrants from Eastern Europe, North Africa, and Arab nations also wear their own traditional clothing.

Schools and Universities

Education is very important to all Greek parents. They see education as a means for their children to get a good job, which often means work in an Athens office. City jobs are much sought-after, and many people from the Greek countryside leave farms to find work in Athens.

Every child between the ages of six and fifteen in Athens must attend school. Children start at elementary school and, at the age of twelve, go to junior school (like junior high school). All state-run schools are free. Athens also has several well-known private schools where pupils must pay fees unless they gain a scholarship. Among these schools are the famous Philekpaideftiki Etaireia on Panepistimiou Street and the Ellinogermaniki Agogi on Chalandri Street.

Students study a mixture of modern and classic subjects, including computers, the

▼ *These children are studying at an elementary school. The school day usually ends at 1:00 P.M.*

▲ *The University of Athens was founded in 1837. It was the first university in the Greek nation.*

English language, and ancient Greek literature and history. Students visit many local sites to learn about Greek history. Religion is also an important school subject.

When students leave junior school, many of them go on to a college or high school where they prepare for university entrance exams and studies. Athens has many universities. The most well-known universities include the University of Athens, which offers courses in economics, theology, philosophy, law, and science, and the National Technical University, with courses in engineering and other related subjects.

Teenage Trends

Teenagers in Athens follow the fashions of Europe and the United States. They enjoy wearing stylish clothes and listening to rock and hip-hop music — although most teens also love traditional Greek music. In summer, many teenagers go to clubs near the beaches of Glyfada, where they can dance in the open air. Teens mostly get to the clubs by way of buses or trains. No one can drive a car in Greece before the age of eighteen.

At eighteen, boys reach a special milestone in their lives: they are required to serve for twelve months in the armed forces. University students, however, can delay their service until after graduation.

Watch Out for Sharks!

Schoolchildren in Athens often play a game called sharks. Two children act as sharks, while the ground is the "sea," and mats serve as boats. The two sharks try to catch the other children, who have to keep moving from mat to mat in search of food. If four children stand on a mat at the same time, it will "sink." If a child is caught in the "sea," he or she is out of the game.

Athens at Work

Throughout nearly all of its history, Greece has been a land of farmers. The vast majority of people worked in agriculture. Today this picture is dramatically different because over half of the Greek population works in what are called "service" industries, such as tourism and finance. The headquarters of this huge commercial world is the city of Athens. Employees in the public sector work an average of thirty-nine hours a week, with twenty days of vacation per year. Greece has a national minimum wage that is fixed through an agreement between employers and unions.

Money and Markets

As an economic center, Athens is in an ideal position. Its location between Europe and Asia on the Mediterranean coast has helped the city grow into an important trading link between the continents, particularly in recent years. The city's strong influence in the region is illustrated through the Athens Stock Exchange — the ups and downs in this market are often felt by the economies of neighboring countries.

In 2001, the Athens Stock Exchange was recognized as a strong and important stock exchange in Europe. The exchange has also modernized. All trading is now done electronically, and the old trading floor of

◀ *A fisherman tends his boat in Piraeus harbor. A wide variety of fish are caught in Greek waters.*

▲ *Greeks are avid newspaper readers. Newsstands
like this one are common on the streets of Athens.*

the nineteenth-century exchange building is now used for exhibitions and lectures.

Central Athens contains banks and insurance firms, as well as the headquarters of Greece's major companies. The National Bank of Greece, for example, stands on Syntagma Square. Athens also has many agencies dealing in the export of Greek goods through the city's airports and the port of Piraeus. These businesses all need and employ accountants, tax advisers, and computer experts.

The Media

Athens is the center of many national media outlets in Greece. Greece has nearly twenty major national newspapers, including an English-language newspaper. All of the national papers are printed and published in Athens.

Several state-run radio stations, as well as local commercial radio stations, are broadcast from the city. The Greek government also runs two television stations. The programming on commercial television stations, however, is more popular. Many of these commercial stations offer satellite and cable broadcasts.

The Greek Trireme

The ancient Athenian navy had one of the deadliest warships of its time — the trireme. Three banks, or sets, of oarsmen powered the boat fast enough to reach the quick speeds necessary to ram enemy ships and sink them. In 1987, a replica of a trireme was built in Piraeus to discover exactly how these vessels worked. It took 170 oarsmen to power this reconstruction, called the Olympias. *Now kept in Phaleron Bay, the* Olympias *has become a tourist attraction.*

Imports and Exports
More than half of all Greece's industrial products are made in the Greater Athens area. The city has over 50,000 companies that range in size from employing just a handful of people to employing thousands. The exporting of locally produced goods is a vital part of the Greek economy, and a large amount of these goods travel through the port of Piraeus. Now that Greece is part of the European Union (E.U.), its most important trade partners are other E.U. countries, especially Germany and Italy.

Factories and Refineries
The many factories around Piraeus and Eleusis Bay produce a huge variety of products. Cement and other construction materials have been produced here for over one hundred years. Factories also process and package home-grown food and tobacco for export. Workers also weave, cut, and stitch clothes and textiles. Thousands of smaller workshops produce traditional goods in metal, wood, and leather.

The largest sector of Athenian industry is chemicals. Giant tankers from the east bring petroleum, which is refined and made into many materials including jet fuel and fuel for home heating furnaces.

Masters of the Sea
Piraeus is one of the busiest ports on the Mediterranean Sea. Over 10 million tons of goods flow in and out of the port each year, a figure which includes most of the country's exports and imports. Also Piraeus is home to the vast fleet of Greek merchant ships that carry much of this trade. With more than 3,000 vessels, the Greek fleet is now the largest merchant fleet in the world.

Athenians have been famous for many centuries for their shipbuilding skills. Today, the shipbuilding industry in Piraeus is still large, although it is struggling to compete with rivals in Southeast Asia. Some 5,000 people work in local shipyards. One of the largest shipyards is Elefsina, which constructs ships for the Greek navy as well as bridges, slipways, floating platforms, and even railroad cars.

Moving Around Athens
Driving in Athens can be difficult and frustrating. A huge volume of traffic often clogs city streets, and road construction or

▲ *This shipyard is in Piraeus harbor. Greece has one of the largest fleets of merchant ships in the world.*

political demonstrations and strikes can also cause delays. Congestion problems, however, are improving in the city, thanks to new roads and improved public transportation systems.

Above and Below Ground
Usually packed with passengers, Athens's blue city buses have been battling their way through the streets of central Athens for decades. They run every fifteen minutes from early morning to midnight, and the fare costs the same for any journey. Athenians buy their tickets in advance from stores and newsstands. Trolleybuses (electric buses linked to overhead cables) also serve the city center, and express buses link the city to the airports and the port of Piraeus.

Yellow taxis are cheap because the fares are fixed at a low rate by the Greek government. Taxi drivers often try to increase their earnings by carrying more than one set of passengers at a time and having them all pay separately.

Athens also has a metro rail system. A single metro line connects the port of Piraeus via twenty-two stations with northern Athens. Two additional lines have recently been added in preparation for the 2004 Olympic Games.

Getting Out of Athens
Located at the intersection of Europe and Asia, Athens is a major destination on the international travel network. Rail, sea, and air links to Athens from abroad are efficient.

▲ *Passengers board one of the city's famous blue and white buses.*

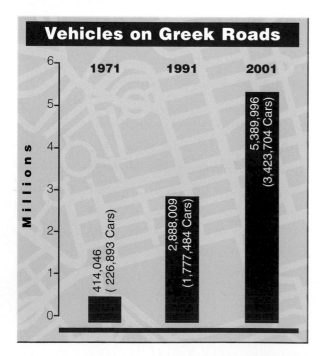

Vehicles on Greek Roads

1971   1991   2001

Millions

414,046 (226,893 Cars)

2,888,009 (1,777,484 Cars)

5,389,996 (3,423,704 Cars)

Athens has been the site of Greece's main international airport for many years. Until recently, Ellinikon was the main airport. In 2001, however, the modern Eleftherios Venizelos Airport opened to prepare for the flood of visitors to the 2004 Athens Olympics. Ellinikon has since closed. The new airport expects eventually to handle over 16 million passengers a year.

Two railroad stations are located side by side in central Athens. Larissis Station handles mainline trains arriving from northern Greece and neighboring countries, while Peloponnese Station caters to train travel coming mainly from the east.

◀ *The number of vehicles using Greek roads continues to increase every year.*

Ferry boats travel from Piraeus to the Greek islands and ports on the Greek mainland, as well as to the eastern coast of Italy and ports on the Mediterranean Sea. Faster hydrofoils take passengers to closer destinations in the Saronic Gulf or on the Peloponnese peninsula.

Tourism

In 2001, over 14 million tourists visited Greece. Most of these tourists arrived in Athens. Many pass through the city on their way to other vacation destinations, but a large number take time to see the sights of Athens. Tourism is a major industry (well

Beating the Car Ban

In 1982, a law geared to reduce car use in Athens went into effect. On days with even dates only cars with license plates ending in even numbers could drive into the city center. Cars with plates ending in odd numbers were permitted on odd dates. The law should have cut the amount of traffic in half, but it didn't. Many Athenian families simply kept two cars, one with an even- and one with an odd-numbered plate.

▼ *Tourists climb the steps to the Propylaia, the ancient entrance to the Acropolis.*

The National Archaeological Museum

The National Archaeological Museum on Patission Street houses one of the greatest collections of ancient Greek art in the world. The collection is so huge that it would take several days just to see everything. Visitors can view an amazing array of the jewelry, weapons, sculptures, wall-paintings, and pottery of several eras, from prehistoric to Roman times and beyond. World famous treasures on display here include the gold mask of Agamemnon and the Warrior Vase.

over one million people a year visit the Acropolis alone), and the industry has had a huge impact on daily life in Athens. The city has thousands of hotels and guest-houses, as well as restaurants, stores, and special facilities that cater to tourists.

The tourist industry employs thousands of Athenians, including tour bus drivers, travel agents, guides, and interpreters. The tourist season still peaks in spring and summer, but the city is now promoting year-round tourism. A longer tourist season will not only increase the amount of money that foreigners spend in Athens, but it also will safeguard the jobs of those people in the tourism industry who have little work during the winter months.

Pollution Problems

A soaring population, along with the tourism boom, has put enormous pressure on housing, hotels, and other public facilities in Athens. The large population combined with tourism also produces a

▼ *Air quality reports have some good news for Athenians. The levels of four dangerous pollutants in the atmosphere appear to be decreasing.*

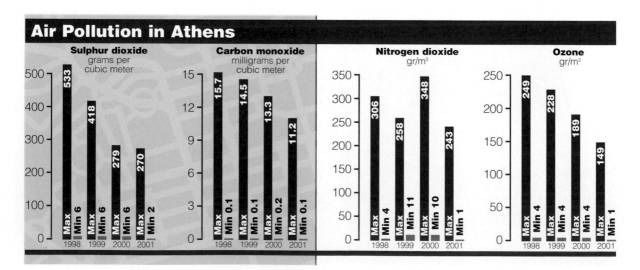

Air Pollution in Athens

Sulphur dioxide (grams per cubic meter)

Year	Max	Min
1998	533	6
1999	418	6
2000	279	6
2001	270	2

Carbon monoxide (milligrams per cubic meter)

Year	Max	Min
1998	15.7	0.1
1999	14.5	0.1
2000	13.3	0.2
2001	11.2	0.1

Nitrogen dioxide (gr/m³)

Year	Max	Min
1998	306	4
1999	258	11
2000	348	10
2001	243	1

Ozone (gr/m³)

Year	Max	Min
1998	249	4
1999	228	4
2000	189	4
2001	149	1

▲ *A haze of polluted air darkens the sky over Athens. Air pollution can cause health problems.*

staggering mass of vehicles that jam the streets. Vehicle exhaust, together with the fumes produced by refineries and factories, has created a major air pollution problem in Athens. For many days of the year, a thick cloud of smog hangs over the city.

The effects of pollution on the city are devastating. Air pollution not only causes health problems such as asthma, it also combines with rainwater to create acid rain. Acid rain is slowly destroying the ancient monuments that tourists come to Athens to see. Many statues and monuments have been replaced with concrete replicas while the originals are stored safely in museums.

Government

Athens has been the seat of Greece's national government for many years. The Parliament building on Syntagma Square was once the home of the Greek royal family and still has an honor guard standing proudly outside. Major government offices, embassies of foreign countries, the seat of the Archbishop of Athens, and the country's Supreme Court are also housed in the city.

Mayor and Council

Greece is split into thirteen regions, and Athens is the chief city of the Attica Region. The regions of Greece are divided further into prefectures. The Athens-Piraeus prefecture includes many smaller municipalities. The residents of each municipality elect a mayor and council to govern them. Everybody aged eighteen and older can vote. In elections for the national parliament everybody eligible to vote is required to vote by law.

The mayor of Athens is aided by a council committee of about forty members.

▼ *Posters for rival political parties line the streets during a national election. The Greek Parliament has three hundred elected deputies, or members.*

The council has several departments that run various aspects of city government, from finance and legal affairs to public relations.

The mayor and the council decide how the city's money will be raised and spent and are responsible for the health and welfare of the people who live in Athens. They organize health centers, services for the homeless, centers offering advice and care for drug users, and many other social

"The new century will find Athens more modern, more elegant, friendlier toward both its citizens and its visitors, more harmonious and brighter."

—Dimitris Avramopoulos, mayor of Athens, 2001.

services. To encourage people to exercise, the council runs many outdoor sports centers and children's playgrounds, as well as public gyms and swimming pools.

Keeping law and order is the job of the Athens police. They are part of the new national Hellenic Police Force and are closely connected with the Greek army. Athens also has a special force of Tourist Police whose job is to protect and give help to foreign visitors.

Palace and Parliament

The Old Palace, or Parliament building, stands on the west side of the National Garden. This grand building was completed around 1842 to house King Otto and his successors. In the 1920s, the royal family moved to the Nea Anaktora, or New Palace, which was built in 1898 on east side of the National Garden. Today both palaces have new uses. The Old Palace is now the home of the Greek Parliament, while the New Palace is the official residence of the President of Greece. The Greek royal family has been living abroad since the country became a republic in 1974. The palaces are guarded by special soldiers called evzones (above). Their flamboyant marching and traditional costume (pleated skirt, tasselled cap, and thick stockings) make them a popular tourist attraction.

CHAPTER 5

Athens at Play

Nights are busy and long in Athens. Athenians like to stay up late. They have many ways to enjoy their time off, from simply strolling in the streets and visiting friends to eating in restaurants, watching movies, or dancing in clubs. Plenty of tavernas and coffee bars stay open until the early hours of the morning, and the roads are always crowded with traffic.

The Outdoors and Movies

Athens in midsummer is hot, even at night. Not surprisingly as much entertainment as possible takes place outdoors. Several open-air movie theaters, such as Sine Pari in Plaka and Thissio near the Acropolis, operate during the summer months and are popular meeting places for young Athenians. Indoor movie theaters are even easier to find, and dozens can be found in the city center alone.

The Theater of Dionysus

The theater of Dionysus (lower left), one of the oldest theaters in the world, lies on the southern side of the Acropolis. Dating from the fifth century B.C., the theater's stone seats rise in curved rows on three sides. It once had sixty-four of these rows, to seat some 17,000 spectators. The works of three great local playwrights — Aeschylus, Sophocles, and Euripides — were first performed here in about 450 B.C.

Traditional and Popular Music

The central areas are also full of discos and night clubs, although the largest ones can be found near the old Ellenikon airport and along the coast east of Piraeus. The clubs offer live and recorded music covering everything from hip-hop to Greek traditional music. Many of these clubs, however, are largely aimed at attracting foreign tourists.

Greek rock and jazz draw small audiences, but the city is famous for its staging of classical concerts, ballets, and operas, notably at the Megaro Mousikis Athinon and the Olympia Theater. Countless venues also offer traditional folk music, including clubs devoted to *rembetika*. Rembetika is a sort of Greek blues song accompanied by the stringed bouzouki, an instrument similar to the guitar. The rembetika clubs most popular among Athenians include Boemissa in Exarhia, Aptaliko on Ironda Street, and Stoa Athenon near the Central Market. Many music clubs in Athens close down during the very hot months of summer.

Ancient and Modern

Athens is the home of Greek drama, both old and new. The ancient plays of the "Classical Age" — originally written in the ancient Greek language — are regularly staged in Athens, especially during the summer Athens Festival. The works of Sophocles, Aeschylus, and others are

"In the sunlight she [Athens] glitters like a diamond; in the dark she sparkles with a million winking lights."

—Henry Miller, American writer, 1941.

performed in modern Greek in sensational settings such as the classical theater at nearby Epidauros or on a stage on the south slope of the Acropolis. Modern drama is also very popular and is offered at venues ranging from tiny innercity theaters to disused quarries on the Athens's outskirts.

Sports

Long evenings and warm summers give the people of Athens plenty of opportunities to enjoy outdoor sports and activities. The nearby coastline encourages swimming, windsurfing, scuba diving, and of course sailing. Athens has one golf course near the old airport and several public tennis courts in the city, but neither golf nor tennis has a large following. Hiking and cycling have recently started to become popular, but they most likely will not catch up with the real national obsessions— soccer and basketball.

Greeks are crazy about soccer. Whether Athenians are playing it or just watching it, soccer is easily the most popular sport. Athens is the country's soccer center and home to at least two-thirds of the clubs in Greece's First Division. The two most famous teams are Olympiakos, which has

ranked as Greek champion over thirty times, and Panathinaikos, a team that has performed well in the European Champions League. Olympiakos plays at Piraeus, while the Panathinaikos stadium is in central Athens near Lykavittos.

Basketball has recently become a favorite sport, and teams from Athens have been very successful in European competitions. The leading teams are also Olympiakos and Panathinaikos.

Another sport that draws large crowds is horse-racing. Races are held three times a week at Athens's Faliron Hippodrome.

Green Spaces

For Athenians who need a break from the bustle of city streets, Athens offers three large parks. The National Garden and the nearby Zappion Gardens have spacious walkways and trees that offer shade from the heat of the sun. Areos Park is a lush, open green space just north of the city center. The park features statues of heroes from the Greek War of Independence.

◀ *Soccer is the most popular spectator sport in Greece. The national team (in red and white here), however, has played in only one World Cup final.*

Light Shows

Each night between April and October a light and sound show is held on the Acropolis. The show is best seen from nearby hills. Athenians are very proud of their heritage and historical sights, although the sights are usually so crowded with tourists that locals rarely visit them except during more peaceful winter months.

Museums

Athens contains some of the most wonderful ancient remains in the world as well as a treasury of sculptures, paintings, and other works kept in museums.

Among notable museums are the Acropolis, the Ancient Agora, the Benaki Museum, the Byzantine Museum, the Jewish Museum, the National Archaeological Museum, the Museum of Greek Folk Art in Plaka, and the National Historical Museum near Syntagma Square, which has a collection of items from the Greek War of Independence.

▼ *The National Garden lies in front of the Zappion, an exhibition hall built in the 1870s.*

CHAPTER 6

Looking Forward

Athens has grown at an amazing rate in the last fifty years. The population of the metropolitan area is now three times greater, and more than 50,000 businesses, ranging from vast shipyards to small workshops, are based in the city. The number of tourists increases every year, bringing more income into the city. The city's growth and popularity, however, has led to a number of problems, including air and water pollution.

Tackling Pollution

Since the early 1980s, Athens's city leaders and the Greek government have made slow progress in tackling air pollution. Taxis and private cars are now banned on specific days from some streets and squares in the center of Athens. Stores and offices have varied working hours, so people are not going to work or leaving for home at the exact same times. Most of the city's power is now generated using natural gas, which is cleaner than the previously used fuels, such as coal.

The Olympics and Beyond

In 1997, Athens was chosen to host the 2004 Olympic Games. The event has attracted a tidal wave of fresh visitors (not to mention competitors and officials). The council and government built new facilities, including an Olympic Village for 17,000

◄ *These boys will see huge changes in their city as buildings and communications are modernized.*

The First Olympics

The very first Olympic Games took place in 776 B.C. at Olympia in western Greece. The games were held every four years until they were banned in A.D. 394. It was another 1,500 years before the Olympics began again, thanks to the energy and vision of a Frenchman, Baron Pierre de Coubertin. He helped organize the first modern Olympics, staged in Athens in 1896. Athens's most popular winner that year was a Greek runner who came first in the marathon.

"The new Athens Municipal Council sees the 2004 Olympic Games not as an end but as a beginning of a maturing and upgraded Athens."

—Dora Bakoyianni, mayor of Athens, 2002.

athletes at the base of Mount Parnitha, a sailing center at Agios Kosmas, baseball and softball fields, a complex for boxing, an equestrian center, an Olympic rowing center, a complex for volleyball, a complex for handball and Taekwondo, and a canoe/kayak slalom center. Some 125 miles (200 km) of road have been built or upgraded and include a link to the city's new international airport. The city's metro system also is currently being renovated and extended. All of these new facilities not only will serve the Olympic events but also will improve Athens's appeal as a tourist destination.

Other projects for the future include unifying and improving green areas and building new parks, placing new parking lots underground, increasing bus services from outlying areas to rail and metro stations, and expanding the municipal police force.

▼ *The first Olympic Games of the modern era were held in Panathenaic Stadium in 1896.*

Time Line

B.C.

ca.1900 Greek peoples have settled in Attica.

ca.1400 Royal fortress built on Acropolis.

ca.800–682 City ruled by kings.

ca.650 Athens is Greece's most important city, ruled by rich, powerful archons.

560 Peisistratos seizes power and becomes first "tyrant."

510 Last tyrant, Peisistratos's son Hippias, is expelled from Athens.

508 Reforms under Cleisthenes; beginnings of democracy.

490 Athenians defeat invading Persians at Marathon.

480 Second Persian invasion; Athenian victory at Salamis.

461 Pericles becomes leader; Classical Age of Athens; building of the Parthenon.

431–404 Peloponnesian War between Athens and Sparta ends in defeat for Athens.

336–323 Alexander the Great rules all Greece.

146 Athens becomes part of the Roman province of Greece.

A.D.

50 Saint Paul preaches in the city; the coming of Christianity.

267 Athens sacked by Germanic tribes.

529 Byzantine rule; Byzantine emperor closes Athens universities.

1018 Byzantine Emperor Basil II visits Athens.

1456 Ottomans conquer Athens; Turkish rule begins.

1687 Venetian shell damages the Parthenon.

1801 Lord Elgin loots carvings from the Acropolis.

1821 Greek War of Independence begins; Athens captured by Greek rebels.

1826 Turks recapture city.

1833 Turks leave Athens.

1834 King Otto makes Athens the Greek capital.

1896 Athens hosts the first Olympic Games of the modern era.

1923 Greece defeated in Balkans War; 300,000 refugees settle in Athens area.

1941 Germany invades Greece and occupies Athens.

1944 Germans withdraw from city; Greek civil war begins.

1949 End of civil war; communists defeated.

1950 onwards Industrial expansion sees rapid growth of Piraeus area.

1967–74 Greece ruled by military group called the "colonels."

1973 Student protests in Athens against military colonels' rule.

1981 Greece joins the European Community (later European Union).

1999 Earthquake kills 138 people and leaves 70,000 homeless.

2004 Athens hosts Olympic Games.

Glossary

accountant a person who keeps or checks the financial records of a business or person.

archaeologists scientists who study the remains of ancient civilizations.

archons nine governing officials who ruled ancient Athens at one time in its history.

city-state a state, or self-ruling area, that consists of a city and its outlying territory.

Classical Age in Athens, the period in ancient Athenian culture lasting from about B.C. 450 to 404. Philosophy and the arts flourished during this time.

communists people who believe that the people of a country should own the country's wealth and property in common.

European Union a commercial and political association of many European countries, including Greece.

flea market a market where a variety of inexpensive items are sold by private traders.

frieze a decorated or carved horizontal band on the upper part of a wall.

hydrofoil a fast boat with underwater fins. The boat rises up out of the water onto the fins when it reaches a certain speed.

medieval dating from the Middle Ages, roughly between the fall of the Roman Empire in the 400s and the Renaissance in the mid-1400s.

metropolitan area the whole region of a very large or important city.

military rule the governing of a country by the armed forces, led by its chief officers.

Muslim a person who follows the Islamic faith, believing in Allah as the only god and Mohammad as his prophet.

peninsula a piece of land surrounded by water on three sides.

Persia an ancient kingdom based in modern-day Iran that existed until around the seventh century and eventually evolved into modern-day Iran.

philosopher a person who seeks, through deep study and contemplation, the truths and meaning of life and the universe.

refugee someone who flees his/her native land and seeks a safe place in another land.

resurrection rising from the dead.

service industry an area of work that is based on providing care for or meeting the needs of others, rather than producing goods. Workers in the service industry include nurses, bankers, and bus drivers.

Steppes vast, level plains of southeastern Europe and Asia.

stock money or other wealth that a business raises by selling "shares," or pieces, of its ownership through a stock exchange, or trade.

suburb a community or development on the edge of a city.

textile cloth or fabric usually made from woven threads.

tyrant a ruler who takes power and governs a land without consulting the wishes of the people.

Further Information

Books

Connolly, Peter and Hazel Dodge. *The Ancient City: Life in Classical Athens and Rome.* Oxford University Press, 2000.

Dubin, Marc S. *Greece: Athens and the Mainland: Eyewitness Travel Guides.* Dorling Kindersley, 2003.

Honan, Linda. *Spend the Day in Ancient Athens: Projects and Activities that Bring the Past to Life.* John Wiley and Sons, 1998.

Kotapish, Dawn. *Daily Life in Ancient and Modern Athens.* Lerner, 2003.

Shuter, Jane. *The Acropolis. Visiting the Past* series. Heinemann Library, 2000.

Stein, Conrad R. *Athens. Cities of the World* series. Children's Press, 1997.

Willett, David, and Kim Wildman. *Lonely Planet: Athens.* Lonely Planet, 2001.

Web sites

www.athens.olympic.org
Athens's official 2004 Olympic Games web site.

www.culture.gr
The Greek Ministry of Culture's guide to Greek culture and the museums of Athens.

www.greece-athens.com
Guide to the city.

www.gnto.gr
Greek National Tourism Organization web site.

www.greece.gr/CITY_GUIDES/index.htm
Athens city guide produced by Greece Now, an online magazine

www.travelling.gr/helloathens/
Travel guide for the city.

www.indiana.edu/~kglowack/athens/
Photos and descriptions of Athens historical sites

Index

Page numbers in **bold** indicate pictures.